THE
CALL CENTRE C… …RE
POCKETBOO…

By Mike Applegarth, Adrian … Posner

Drawings by Phil Hailstone

"Technology is becoming increasingly important in the business environment. However, ultimately it doesn't matter how good the technology is, it is people who make the real difference. This book is a distillation of considerable experience, which reflects the customer service issues in our modern world. Concise and easy to read, it is excellent for anyone involved in any aspect of customer service."

Jonathan Blain, Chief Executive Officer, ASAP International Group Plc

Published by:
Management Pocketbooks Ltd
Laurel House, Station Approach, Alresford, Hants SO24 9JH, U.K.
Tel: +44 (0)1962 735573   Fax: +44 (0)1962 733637
E-mail: sales@pocketbook.co.uk
Website: www.pocketbook.co.uk

First edition published in 2001 as The E-customer Care Pocketbook.
This edition published 2005.

British Library Cataloguing-in-Publication Data – A catalogue record for this book is available from the British Library.

ISBN 1 903776 33 3

Design, typesetting and graphics by **efex ltd**.   Printed in U.K.

Who should read this book?

Primarily, this book is for all staff dealing with customers over the telephone or via the internet, whether or not they regard themselves as working in a call centre or for a dot.com organisation.

If that is you, you will not only be offered guidelines and practical ideas for enhancing the customer service you directly provide, but you will also gain an insight into the support mechanisms and further technology available to help your cause. It will enable you to see where you fit within an overall customer service strategy.

There are also issues for managers of call centres or dot.coms to address, so they too will find this book helpful.

The book does not tell you how to set up a website, but it does explore some design issues and reviews the customer service pitfalls of the modern age.

CONTENTS

INTRODUCTION

INTRODUCTION

A NEW REVOLUTION

Here we are at the turn of another century. With each new century we have entered a new era. There was the Agricultural Revolution at the start of the 18th Century, the Industrial Revolution at the start of the 19th Century, and the 'communications' revolution (the telephone) at the start of the 20th Century.

What revolution awaits us this time? The internet and mobile communications are having a dramatic effect on the way we lead our lives. People's buying practices are changing, and with this the *customer revolution* is underway. The importance of customer service is fast emerging. Now, the mass media creates the awareness and the customers come to you: it's less to do with *selling*, more to do with *helping customers buy from you, again and again!*

INTRODUCTION

DOT.COMMERCE

The dot.com boom has brought convenience to window-shopping and all but removed the *closed* signs.

Traditionally, the main contact with customers was face-to-face. However, economic pressures have led to the telephone line being the backbone of customer service for large companies.

Often when a new method of communication arrives, we believe it will replace existing methods (photographs for paintings, telephone for post, television for cinema, internet for everything!). More commonly it just adds to the mix.

In this book we explore the ways in which customers who have come to us could still be lost, and what we must do to keep them and get their friends aboard as well.

CUSTOMER PROMISCUITY

Customers equipped with today's technology find it easy to move from one dot.com shop to the next, or one call centre to the next, so *lock-in* is important. Nowadays, customers are promiscuous: they have little loyalty and will not waste their time and effort doing business with you if another supplier makes it easier for them. Time is something that can always be spent elsewhere, along with the money.

INTRODUCTION

AFTER SALES SERVICE

Some companies seem to provide the 'shop window' that customers want. But having promised to deliver, the only support they provide is in getting the customer's back up, whereas they should be **giving** the customer back-up!

What follows is a true story about one customer whose time and money could certainly have been spent better elsewhere. It concerns a major high street computer retailer who purports to be able to construct personal computers to the customer's specification. The following events reflect that company's concept of customer service and is exactly what this book aims to put right.

Gateway to Hell!

We start when the high street store confirmed details of the required computer and promised delivery within 7 – 10 days. Payment was taken by credit card and the customer went home happy with her purchase, anticipating the advantage it would give to her home-based business.

AFTER SALES SERVICE

A call from the customer to check the likely delivery date revealed no apparent problems. But on the seventh day the store rang to say that the computer could not be built to the agreed specification. An internal zip drive could not be included, therefore the price would be lower and a new payment authority required. The computer could not be built until the authority was received! To cut a long story short, delivery took five weeks.

But that was only the start! Printers and peripheral equipment never worked properly with the computer and so the customer sought help from the store. Its reaction was to send a contracted engineer, who incidentally had installed the machinery originally, to resolve the problem. The customer had to pay £20 per hour for the privilege!

AFTER SALES SERVICE

Further problems surfaced. Not trusting the engineer, nor wanting to pay further, the customer found a support number and was connected to a call centre in the States. They guided her through a process of shutting down software, as the computer's resources were inexplicably overloading. Unfortunately, and unbeknown to the customer, the scanner was disabled during that process and, later, could not be used to complete an important business document by its deadline. The customer was left to panic and incur additional expense again by doing creative things with pay-as-you-use photocopiers. Solving one problem had simply started another.

The next time the customer called the support number, she got an entirely different accent at the end of the line. Her call wasn't routed to the States this time but to another English speaking country where the words can be difficult to discern until the ear becomes attuned to the accent. This time she was told that whoever she had spoken to before had given her the wrong instructions!

AFTER SALES SERVICE

When the CD-rewriter also failed to function properly, all the customer wanted, having spent nearly £2000, was a new machine – one that did the job it was supposed to do. But no! The customer didn't come first: the company's internal processes were more important. The standard reply to any request for a competent engineer to come on site and sort out the computer, or even to provide a temporary replacement while it was being fixed, was *We don't operate that way!*

The customer perceived that her business was at the mercy of an unsympathetic, self-focused, money-grabbing organisation that failed to meet its obligations to her. Not once did anyone express so much as an apology or concern for her predicament. It wasn't just a home PC she was buying, it was also a business tool, offering the hope of greater efficiency and professionalism and contributing to paying the mortgage.

Further insult was added to injury when arrangements were eventually made for the computer to be collected and taken away for repair. The customer had to manage without it for a few days. Needless to say no replacement or compensation were offered.

AFTER SALES SERVICE

Moreover, the courier acting on the manufacturer's behalf went to the wrong address, despite specific instructions from the customer. Although only four miles away, the courier told her the collection would have to be rescheduled for another day!

The convenience of telephony had taken over. After sales service was to be done over the phone and face-to-face contact had to be paid for. Communications were to be remote, leaving the customer feeling very isolated.

The purpose of this story is to show that customer service is measured ultimately by the customer. Customer service cannot exist only at the point of sale. Neither is it a system or set of procedures with an internal focus that views the customer as an irritation and incidental. It is an ethos, a living culture within the organisation, and not just two easy-to-use words – one for each finger!

Inevitably, one disappointed customer's story will deter many other would-be purchasers. Yet that's just the tip of the iceberg now that customers have the choice. It's incidents like this that should be isolated, rather than the customers they refer to!

CUSTOMER PERCEPTION

A recent survey of bank customers supports the lessons from the previous pages. It highlights that the quality of service has worsened dramatically as the banks shift to internet and telephone operations.

Customers, it seems, are unhappy with the loss of face-to-face contact. In particular, they feel that their needs are taking second place to cost cutting and profits.

The message is that the convenience of 24-hour operations has to be tempered with its limitations. Transmitting *to* someone may be quick, but communicating *with* them, before either party can make appropriate decisions, requires more personal rapport to be established and may need involvement from a number of different people in the organisation.

CUSTOMER SERVICE AS SOLE DIFFERENTIATOR

Utilities companies were the early pioneers of treating customer service as though it were a product itself. This is because there is nothing else to differentiate one gas or electricity supplier from another, as the product is the same.

So CRM (Customer Relationship Management) was born out of the need to differentiate providers. It allows the provider to treat each customer as important whilst interfacing as one coherent operation, rather than as departments of the same organisation operating independently without any apparent communication between one another.

CUSTOMER SERVICE AS SOLE DIFFERENTIATOR

Customer service is a number of experiences, not just one product.

What has not changed is the need to build customer loyalty. A life-long relationship with the customer is, therefore, still the goal of all good companies.

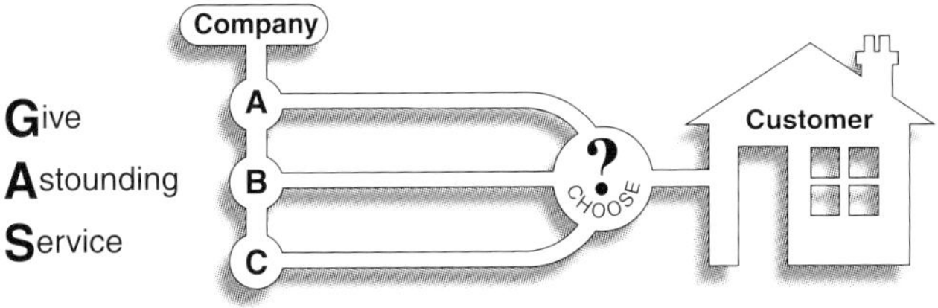

Deregulation of the gas market in the UK has allowed choice for the consumer. The gas product is the same, as is the infrastructure of supply pipelines. What then differentiates the various suppliers? Believe it or not, the unit price per therm is perceived as attributable to the service rather than the product. If a supplier offers more affordable gas with a noticeable level of good customer service, it may have a customer for life.

COMMUNICATION METHODS

ATTITUDE TO CUSTOMERS

Our attitude to customers can be one of irritation or apathy when they don't understand our systems and how we operate. Therefore communication is at the heart of customer service perceptions, and the way we communicate is all-important. Research shows that communication is split into three methods of delivery in normal face-to-face communication:

7% What we say

38% The way we say it

55% Body language

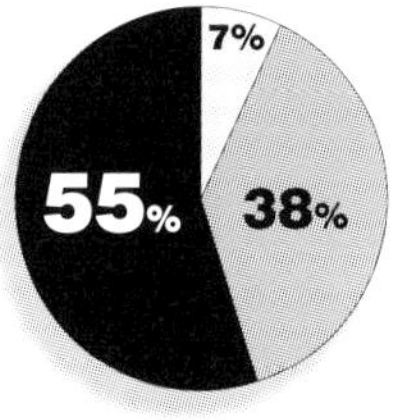

If we cannot see our customers and they cannot see us, then we can rely on only 45% of the medium to communicate our message accurately!

ATTITUDE TO CUSTOMERS

Peter Ustinov defined communication as: *The art of being understood!* How much more chance exists then for misunderstandings and confusion when so much of the visual support of the message – and reaction to it! – is missing?

For example, *fork handles* could easily be misheard as *four candles* or vice versa.

An opera goer might prefer a more formal style of address; a football supporter a more casual approach.

ATTITUDE TO CUSTOMERS

It is well known, and used to good effect by companies, that certain regional accents more readily convey the impression of empathy and understanding. Each country will have its own variations that can be perceived as helpful or unhelpful.

It is certainly unhelpful when a person is confronted by an unfamiliar accent; it can be a struggle to discern the words, especially over the phone. This has become more of an issue now that calls within the UK can be diverted to call centres in America, India or the Republic of Ireland, let alone other parts of the UK. You need to allow for the difficulty callers might have, and you should be prepared to speak more slowly with clearer enunciation of words.

Either way, ensure you are clearly understood and summarise the caller's needs to check and show your own understanding.

WHAT IS A CALL CENTRE?

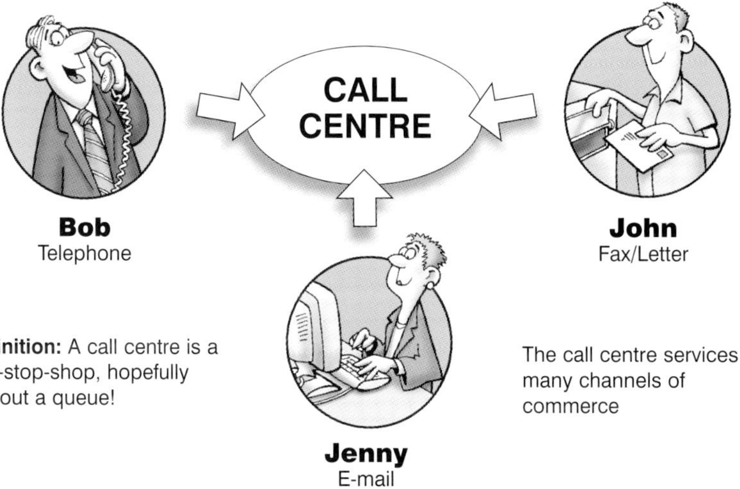

Definition: A call centre is a one-stop-shop, hopefully without a queue!

The call centre services many channels of commerce

CALL CENTRE vs CONTACT CENTRE

We typically use the term *call centre* when referring to communication with the customer. In reality, call centres have traditionally been telephone-based service centres dealing with in-bound calls. A contact centre, on the other hand, deals with all types of customer communication (letter, fax, telephone, e-mail, web chat) and may include out-bound communication too (telesales, etc).

The contact centre faces different workforce scheduling issues. Unlike the phone, e-mail does not usually require an instant response and gaps in phone activity can be used to answer e-mails to help smooth work volumes. This also affects the setting of service levels that customers can expect.

Collecting management information becomes more difficult with more varied activities taking place. The number of phone calls can be taken from the ACD (Automatic Call Distribution), the number of e-mails from statistics held on the internet server, the number of letters/faxes taken from scanners.

As call centres evolve into contact centres handling multimedia interactions there is increasing pressure on workforce management systems to keep up.

A truly effective contact centre will also be skilled in *up-selling* and *cross-selling*.

WHAT TYPE OF CALL CENTRE ARE YOU?

There are two types of call centre:

B2B Business to Business
Here you are likely to have a high volume of web-based activity but a low level of interaction with your call centre. You will need more internet support staff than telephone operators.

B2C Business to Consumer
Here the norm is a low volume of web-based activity per consumer. Because domestic callers tend to be less frequent users of your web service than business users, they are more likely to require assistance from your call centre as issues arise. You will, therefore, need to have a high level of telephone input, with less internet support.

Bob Head, Chief Executive of Smile (the Co-operative Internet Bank) said:

Happy customers will use your internet site, unhappy customers will phone your call centre.

WHAT TYPE OF CALL CENTRE ARE YOU?

CENTRALISED OR LOCALISED?

Many companies have moved to a centralised call centre model, where the customer service facility is located in one place. This may even be based in a different country from where the consumer calls originate (such as in 'Gateway to Hell' in our Introduction). But many customers prefer to talk to someone with *local* knowledge, who understands their language, culture and environment.

It is quite conceivable that as complex telephone line routing (distributed telephony) and workforce planning structures become cheaper, we will see more central organisations with staff working locally (even at home). All calls will be initially routed to one location via one telephone number and then, if necessary, automatically distributed elsewhere.

COMPARING COMMUNICATION METHODS

The most popular methods of communicating with a customer are:

- Automated interactive voice systems
- Kiosks/automated teller machines
- E-mail
- Websites
- Post (letters)
- Fax
- Phone
- Face-to-face
- Short messaging systems (eg: text messages via mobile phone)

On the following pages we look at the advantages and disadvantages of different forms of communication from the:

Contact centre perspective

Customer perspective

You may like to use the tables as a checklist for a facilitated workshop or evaluation of how to provide the best service for customers.

COMPARING COMMUNICATION METHODS

CONTACT CENTRE PERSPECTIVE

Automated Interactive Voice Systems

Advantages	Disadvantages
Low cost	Inhuman for both parties
Directs customer to appropriate department or individual contact	Customers may take their business elsewhere rather than wait an uncertain length of time
The customer has only one telephone number for many services	May not cater for all the options a customer requires

Kiosks/Automated Teller Machines

Advantages	Disadvantages
In operation 24 hours/day	Technology and practicality may limit number of transactions available, eg: cash or only a statement of account
Low cost	May be left idle for long periods or have people queuing impatiently
	More locations to maintain

COMPARING COMMUNICATION METHODS

CONTACT CENTRE PERSPECTIVE

E-mail

Advantages	Disadvantages
Quick and easy to convey messages to customers who have the facility	Often carelessly composed or appears so to customers (fired off and forgotten)
The same message can be sent simultaneously to many customers	Replies from customers can be lost amongst scores of other e-mails
Can send attachments and hyperlinks	Customers may misinterpret the message
	Can't be sure it has been read by the customer

COMPARING COMMUNICATION METHODS

CONTACT CENTRE PERSPECTIVE

Websites

Advantages

- Open 24 hours/day
- Low cost outlet for giving customers information
- Visitors can be shown browser pictures, videos, text, and can interact in a fixed way
- Changes made at one central point, therefore information is accurate for all customers

Disadvantages

- Needs to be highly developed to be interactive and customer friendly
- Download times can dissuade customers from staying online
- Low propensity of browsers to actually purchase over the internet
- You have no idea why 'customers' visited the site
- It has a structured architecture that bends the customer into the system, not the other way round!
- Customer may not wish to give out personal/credit details

COMPARING COMMUNICATION METHODS

CONTACT CENTRE PERSPECTIVE

Post (letters)

Advantages

Permits considered response – time to prepare thoroughly

Easier to use standard formats

Next day delivery

Enclosures may be used to support the message or help the customer, eg: reply envelopes, brochures

Disadvantages

Slower than other media (snail mail)

Takes more time and money to generate and deliver

The customer may think it's a mailshot and it may go unopened in the bin!

It doesn't interact with the customer and will lack adaptability to reactions

Fax

Advantages

Quick

Can be sent to many customers at cheap rate times

Authorising signatures can be accepted on returned faxes from customers

Disadvantages

No guarantee customers have read it, nor that they can read it (quality of print)

The message may fade (literally) over time

Faxes ringing in homes at cheap rate time (5am!) will aggravate customers

COMPARING COMMUNICATION METHODS

CONTACT CENTRE PERSPECTIVE

Phone

Advantages

Instant dialogue with customers to establish and resolve needs

You can change tack during the conversation if required (two-way)

Understanding (yours and the customer's) can be confirmed immediately

Can use a queuing system and monitor calls

The customer can't see you, so you can create the image of an established, professional company

Disadvantages

You may make several calls before you get to speak to the customer

More difficult to record key points of the conversation accurately and completely

More time may be required in providing written confirmation to the customer for their records

Customers are reluctant to buy over the phone without some other form of interaction

COMPARING COMMUNICATION METHODS

CONTACT CENTRE PERSPECTIVE

Face-to-face

Advantages

Personal rapport is more easily established

Handshake allows warmth

What you see of the customer (circumstances, etc) can determine what you offer

You can change tack during the conversation if required (two-way)

Understanding (yours and the customer's) can be confirmed immediately

Disadvantages

Takes more time to meet customers and can be costly, especially if you're doing the travelling

Horn/halo effect may take over, ie: you may take an instant dislike to the customer which impairs the service

Customers coming to you will need to be welcomed and made comfortable

Customers make judgments on the physical environment, which may hinder their doing business with you

Short Messaging Systems

Advantages

Not staff intensive

Low cost and maintenance to transmit to customers

Disadvantages

Limited characters per message

Open to misinterpretation by customers, through brevity

Messages can arrive late owing to network or memory restrictions on mobile phones

COMPARING COMMUNICATION METHODS

CUSTOMER PERSPECTIVE

Now, viewing the communication methods from the **customers' perspective** we can see what they would consider to be the advantages or disadvantages:

Automated Interactive Voice Systems

Advantages	Disadvantages
It's relatively easy to find a phone	The query never seems to fit the available options!
	Tedious and frustrating if the list of options or queuing time is lengthy
	Never seem to get continuity as there always appears to be a different point of contact

COMPARING COMMUNICATION METHODS

CUSTOMER PERSPECTIVE

Kiosks/Automated Teller Machines

Advantages	Disadvantages
Relatively simple to use	May forget pin code or lose card
May find one within a reasonable distance	Can necessitate a queue in the cold
	May have to travel to get to one
	A limited number of transactions are available and it may not offer the choices required at that time

E-mail

Advantages	Disadvantages
Quick and easy, instant communication – fire off at will!	May not have 24hr access to send/receive e-mails
Customers' expectations of required action are raised	Customers' expectations are dashed and they can't be sure when it has been read and acted upon

COMPARING COMMUNICATION METHODS

CUSTOMER PERSPECTIVE

Websites

Advantages

Low cost of accessing company and product information

Able to surf several sites in a short space of time

Disadvantages

Signposts may be different from those customer identifies with

Customer unaware why information requested/how used

Concerns for security of credit card details, etc

May spend time form-filling only to find transaction can't be completed (frustration and anger)

Post (letters)

Advantages

Customers' letters can provide more clout than other media

Likely to get more attention in the office, as most businesses now correspond by e-mail and phone (mobile/land line)

Disadvantages

Takes time and effort to compose and some customers may not feel able to express themselves this way

Can't be sure when it has been read and acted upon, or by whom

Must also make the effort to send it once written!

COMPARING COMMUNICATION METHODS

CUSTOMER PERSPECTIVE

Fax

Advantages

Signatures of authority may be provided on faxed pro-formae or letters, speeding up transactions

Disadvantages

Can't be sure when it has been read and acted upon

Much more prone to the engaged tone

Need to have a hard copy format in the first place

Phone

Advantages

Allows for action to be agreed following interactive discussion of customer needs

Able to access different departments or people through the one call or number

If freephone – no cost

Disadvantages

Can't see the products, forms or company and have only the words and tone to go by

Frustration and anger can arise from becoming lost in the system during transfers

COMPARING COMMUNICATION METHODS

CUSTOMER PERSPECTIVE

Face-to-face

Advantages	Disadvantages
Easier to build rapport and reassurance	Cost of travel, both in terms of time and money
Able to see the scale of the company's operations, products and professionalism	Has to commit to appointments for company representatives coming to visit

Short Messaging Systems

Advantages	Disadvantages
Convenient any time, any place, anywhere (with a signal!)	May take up memory space needed for other messages

It's worth noting that the contact centre's advantage could well be the customer's disadvantage, and vice versa!

IN-HOUSE SYSTEMS

INTEGRATE METHODS

There are advantages or disadvantages inherent in each medium through which we communicate. The same can be said for the way in which the methods are combined.

Most customers want to choose whichever method (or channel) of communication suits them, **varying it at will** during the sales process. Organisations therefore need to integrate channels. For example, customers may order via the internet but make changes to their orders via the telephone to ensure immediate confirmation. The call centre must therefore be able to access the original transactions within seconds of receiving the telephone call.

All channels, then, must be consistent and up-to-date in respect of delivery times.

INTEGRATE CHANNELS

The call centre must be able to access original transactions within seconds of receipt. Therefore, all channels must: **ACCRUE**

Accrue, as defined in the English dictionary, is *to increase by growth or addition, by periodic addition of interest*. Channels must therefore be:

- **A**ccessible - available to everyone
- **C**onsistent - no distortion of information between them
- **C**ost-effective - most efficient to customer and organisation
- **R**eal time - up-to-date and accurate delivery times each moment of the day
- **U**-centred - customers are not third parties: the one in contact is always 'you'
- **E**qually valid - e-mail, fax, phone or letter are equally valid as methods of requesting or delivering a service to/from the customer

CUSTOMER RELATIONSHIP MANAGEMENT (CRM)

CRM is the logical development from ERP (Enterprise Resource Planning). ERP was the realisation of integrating business processes and information so that an enterprise could operate as one unit, rather than as separate departments with separate systems and databases. Consistency and information sharing became the order of the day.

CRM takes this a step further by offering access to customer information to all necessary parts of the business. There are no longer different records kept in different departments; subject to levels of authority and confidentiality they can be shared.

Customer service can now be enhanced with the help of a properly designed management information structure. CRM is not software alone, but a combination of software interfacing with a best practice approach. CRM is both a philosophy and a management tool, designed to target and win more business from customers more cost-effectively.

IN-HOUSE SYSTEMS

INTERNAL (ERP)

This provides a single view of suppliers and internal processes.

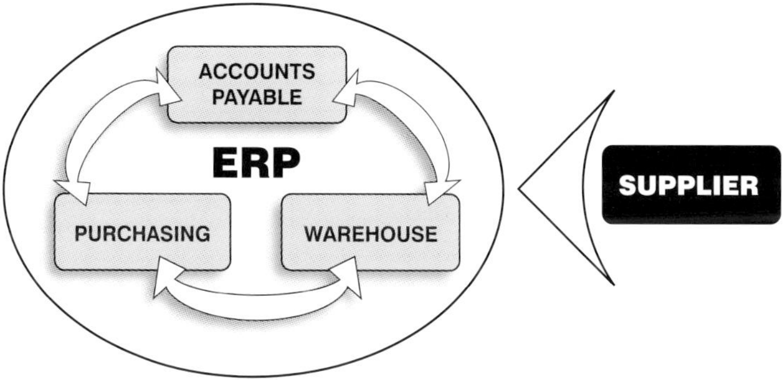

IN-HOUSE SYSTEMS

EXTERNAL (CRM)

This creates a single view of your customer from all parts of the organisation.

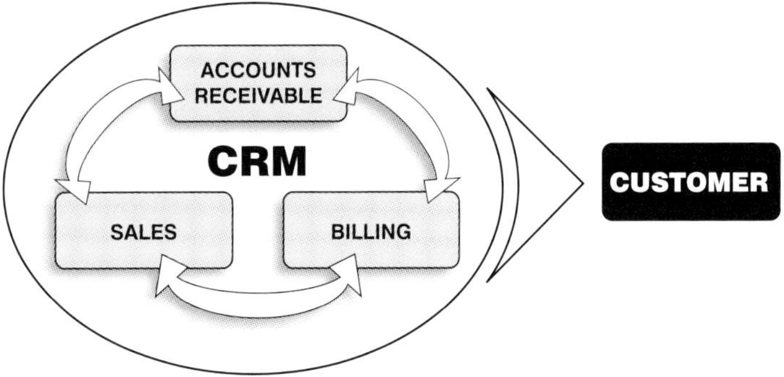

CRM is achievable through the technological advances of the present time.

EFFECTIVE CRM

To function correctly, CRM requires an effective call centre and integrated technology – one-stop shop, so to speak.

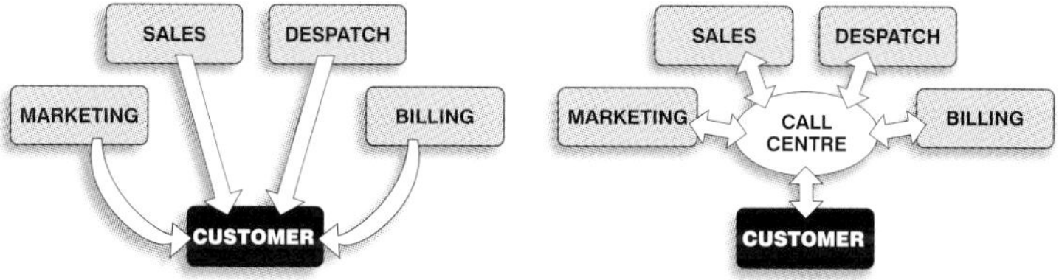

Integrated technology is especially important where several different products are available. Virgin uses one integrated website to offer many diverse services (cars, financial services, travel, books, energy, mobile phones, music and wine). But each is a different business with different call centres, allowing staff to remain experts for that service line. Customers get the best of both worlds – one contact number that allows them to be routed to the area of specialism required.

EFFECTIVE CRM

Customer service is about building better relationships with customers, possibly on a selective basis as there may be certain customers with whom you don't wish to build a relationship.

Yet, CRM is often pushed by CRM vendors as campaign management (if they sell campaign systems) or data warehousing (if they sell data warehouse products) or … and so on. So beware. And don't forget, you'll need to integrate your new CRM into existing systems.

A survey for BT (British Telecom) in November 2000 by The Practice showed CRM increased:

Customer satisfaction	74%	Number of customers	43%
Customer retention	68%	Employee satisfaction	42%
Competitive advantage	61%	Customer profitability	42%
Knowledge management	55%		

Good CRM systems allow you to predict churn (customers leaving you) before it happens by identifying changes in customer behaviour (reductions in spending). This allows you to take pre-emptive action to revive customer business by enhancing the service you provide. However, it's also worth noting that attrition is not bad in all cases (eg: with unprofitable customers).

KNOWLEDGE MANAGEMENT

List the typical information you request from a customer. Compare it with what you would find helpful to know about them, and you will immediately identify whether you have a shortfall in your knowledge management.

As a prompt, the more typical details asked of customers are listed below. They may be acquired through casual conversation or from a questionnaire, perhaps via the telephone or the internet, with optional or mandatory fields.

- Name
- Date of Birth (DoB) – eg: to send birthday cards
- Address and post code
- E-mail address
- Telephone contact number
- Occupation
- Hobbies or interests
- Income indicators
- Family size
- Social activities

Also, ask yourself how you might use the information you acquire. For example, you might wish to send birthday greetings (knowing their DoB) or personalise hospitality events (knowing their hobbies or interests).

BUILD A CUSTOMER DATABASE

Build a database containing valuable profiles of each of your customers – and use it. Such a database can provide organisations with customer knowledge at the touch of a button.

In other circumstances it might take years of direct contact with customers for even one sales person to acquire such knowledge. And when that sales person leaves, often the knowledge goes too!

How frequently do you update or corroborate knowledge on your customer database?

BUILD A CUSTOMER DATABASE

For the database to be effective, all staff must have the discipline to update it after each customer visit (interaction).

Central to CRM is the use of knowledge about customers to either align yourself with them or align them with you! 'Knowledge is Power' goes the adage.

The knowledge must be up-to-date and capable of being categorised for *field sorts*. For example, it should be possible to identify all females between 30 and 45 years of age from the southern region, who like to drive family convertibles and who have an income bracket greater than £20,000 per annum.

BUSINESS INTELLIGENCE

Gathering data does not, in itself, bring it into the realm of consciousness. It cannot, therefore, be regarded as knowledge.

Many people and organisations acquire knowledge every day but don't seem to share it with the right people and apply it. If they did, the business as a whole would be more intelligent.

HOW BUSINESS INTELLIGENCE EVOLVES

The following reflects the evolution of business intelligence:

- Firstly, an organisation acquires **data** on its customers.
- Used correctly, that data will enable the organisation to identify the differences in its customer-base (for example, male versus female and those with bank accounts and those without). This is **information**.
- Identified correctly, the information is used to pinpoint, for example, a customer's location (street?), socio-economic group and buying potential.
- If this **knowledge** is used within the organisation – and then targeted correctly – it provides **business intelligence**. This can be defined as *the infinite number of possibilities for using and interfacing each piece of data to enhance the development of the business by attracting and maintaining customers.*

USING TECHNOLOGY TO PERSONALISE

Some customers may prefer to use e-mail, others will not be web-enabled and may prefer the telephone. Then again some customers feel uncomfortable using the telephone and may prefer talking face-to-face. **It is important to establish which methods of communication your customers prefer** so that you can build in sufficient capability in your call (or contact) centre.

Obviously there will be cost implications. The most expensive method is face-to-face, followed by letter, telephone and, finally, the internet. However, a look at the earlier chapter on Communication Methods will show that cost is not the only consideration.

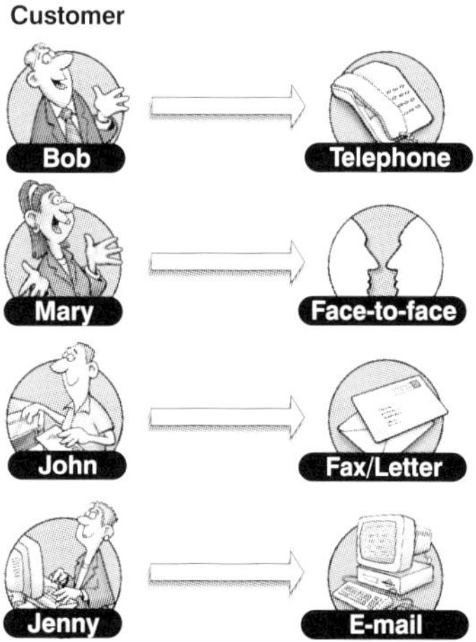

CHECKLIST

Five things your organisation/department needs to know or check before conducting further business with customers:

1. Have they bought before?
2. If *yes*, how much (spend, number, paid, unpaid)?
3. What products (type, quantity) were purchased?
4. How did they pay?
5. What were the delivery addresses and day-time telephone numbers?

This is an example checklist. You may wish to adapt it to suit your own particular needs.

SINGLE VIEW OF YOUR ORGANISATION

Customers want a single view of the organisations they are dealing with. In the banking sector, for example, customers want the same service for current accounts, loans, savings, etc, regardless of the communication method they choose. This means having an organisational structure that supports the new methods (such as e-commerce) and the traditional channels (namely phone and face-to-face) equally well.

Visitors to the Virgin website, for example, can view a range of products (financial services, leisure and various commodity items) all within the one virtual department store. Similarly, amazon.com offers a variety of products (books, videos, CDs, DVDs, etc) within its virtual library.

SINGLE VIEW OF YOUR CUSTOMER

Organisations that adopt a *single view* approach put the customer at the centre of their business processes. They have a system that *talks* to each part of their database. Take an insurance company, for example:

When a customer asks for a home/contents policy it should be possible to identify that a garage is attached to the property. In that case motor insurance can also be offered. A house size of 2, 3 or 4 bedrooms should indicate children, therefore offering health and life assurance products may be of interest. Alternatively, a large house may indicate that the customer is working from home, in which case a business policy may be more relevant. Organisations must think about real cross-selling opportunities such as these.

In insurance markets a customer who has given her date of birth would expect that information to be shared throughout the organisation. Therefore, a 40 year-old with a life insurance policy, who receives a mailshot about a product for cheap healthcare for 70 year-olds, may be put off ever buying another service from that company again. It may also result in the original insurance policy being cancelled. Customers just see the organisation as one entity, and why shouldn't they?!

MANAGEMENT INFORMATION (MI)

It may not be sufficient just to know a customer's personal details and circumstances. You need good MI from your systems, otherwise you may offer promotions to customers who are delinquent payers.

The history of a customer is critical, as it provides the organisation with the intelligence to apply its products and services appropriately. The last transaction on its own is not enough.

Before putting Bob on to the mailshot list, consider if he is disqualified on the following grounds:

- Bad payment record
- Poor credit rating
- Court orders against him

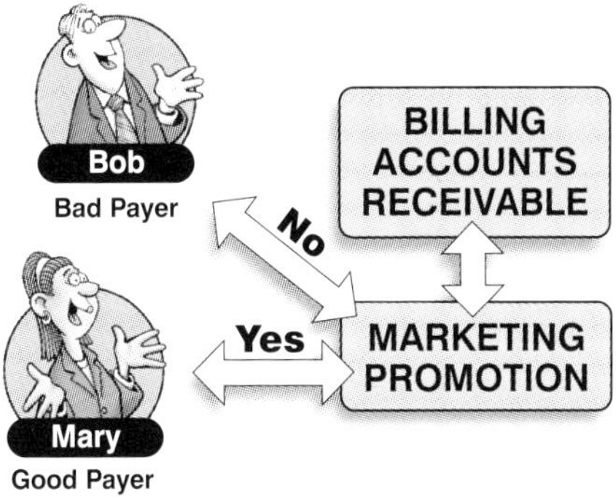

CUSTOMER INTERFACING

PREVENTING CUSTOMER PROMISCUITY

We have already highlighted the promiscuous nature of customers. How can you prevent promiscuity? You have to generate loyalty and make it easy and worthwhile for prospects and customers to contact you. **Think of Promise – Queue – E.T.**

Promise

- Better to *under promise and over achieve*, but seek customer acceptance of what you promise
- Deliver what you have promised
- Show customer there is the promise of good customer service

Queue

- Don't keep them waiting in the system
- Don't have too many layers of keypad options: anything prior to direct, personal contact, is a queue!
- Achieve *one and done* on first contact. Make sure that customer service staff are empowered to resolve the issue.

E.T

- It's alien to many organisations, but phone customers at home (or wherever their contact point is). Why not call them first to keep them informed of what is happening?
- It's good to talk!

TELEPHONE IMAGES

It's worth remembering that whilst we judge ourselves by our intentions, others judge us by our behaviour (what they hear us say and see us do!).

What then are the techniques that can be used over the telephone to create that air of friendliness and professionalism, so that the intention matches behaviour?

Factors contributing to our view of organisations over the telephone can be grouped under the following headings:

- Speed of response and call navigation
- Language
- Control of the call
- Background noise
- Effective use of information

TELEPHONE IMAGES

SPEED OF RESPONSE

To answer within three rings has become the standard, but only if you're ready to deal properly with the call at that time.

Call navigation systems are the order of the day, allowing customers to feel that they are at least in the shop and have perhaps found the store guide. But, callers don't yet know how long the queue is going to be once they've identified where to go.

Above all, avoid telling customers, who have finally reached the end of the queue, that they should have followed another route and will have to repeat their query to someone else.

TELEPHONE IMAGES

LANGUAGE

The obvious contribution of *language* is in the politeness and warmth of the greeting. Callers want to know initially whether they have the correct department; your name, as the recipient, is perhaps not so important at that point. The time to give it is in exchange for obtaining the caller's name. So, *Sales Department, good morning, how may I help?* will progress the call to the next question which may be *And may I have your name please?*

Now the handshake really takes place as the recipient continues with, *My name is Josh, Mrs Brown. Let me see if we have that available*, or whatever would be appropriate. If customers are not ready to listen to a name they won't register it at the start.

You, meanwhile, must be alert to the customer giving his or her name. Listen for it and acknowledge it with the handshake.

TELEPHONE IMAGES

LANGUAGE

As well as the language of warmth and politeness, you need to use the language of benefits.

Customers will more readily accept being transferred if they are told: *We have a department with staff who have specialist knowledge of this issue and they will be able to identify a solution more quickly for you. Do you mind if I transfer you to them?*

In other words, use the phrases that focus on *what's in it for the customer* rather than how much easier it makes life for you and the system!

TELEPHONE IMAGES

LANGUAGE

Best practice will then be for you to pass on the initial information gathered to the person taking the call. If this is not practical (usually because of call waiting) then at least apologise and let the customer know that he or she will have to repeat the information.

Polite use of their name will help customers feel they are being treated as individuals. But don't get too familiar.

Tip: Ring back a sample of customers to check satisfaction. Information from a customer is a gift, so treat it as such.

CUSTOMER INTERFACING

TELEPHONE IMAGES

CONTROL OF THE CALL

Customers like to be confident that the person they are speaking to knows how to deal proficiently with the issue at hand.

Questions take control, and a structured and relevant use of them will instil the necessary confidence. But, it can be lost easily if the customer is asked again for information already given, perhaps in response to an earlier question. People are often so fixed on asking the scripted questions and putting the response in the appropriate data field that they forget to listen.

Let the customer know that you're switched into the call itself and not just to each question in isolation.

Furthermore, don't leave customers hanging on the end of an empty line for longer than two minutes without acknowledging that you haven't forgotten them. It will seem like an eternity to them beyond that and you are likely to have lost control – and, possibly, the call – by the time you return!

TELEPHONE IMAGES

BACKGROUND NOISE

Case Study

A customer phoning a film hire company was told to hold on while the order clerk looked to see if the requested film would be available for the given dates. He then heard the clerk take a puff on a cigarette and say to someone near her that she'd have a coffee. When also asked by her colleague if she had a *punter* on the line, the clerk replied *He can wait, I'm having a break!* Imagine her surprise, after keeping the customer waiting for four minutes, when he asked sarcastically if she'd enjoyed her coffee and cigarette at his expense.

In another environment, a caller on one phone heard a clerk who had put his own call on hold tell his colleague *I've got that 'pain-in-the-a*** Mr x on the phone.* Small world! This caller knew Mr x and was curious how he himself was referred to behind his back!

People are blissfully unaware that earpieces of most modern phones also have microphones in to enhance sound pick-up. Covering the mouthpiece doesn't muffle much!

TELEPHONE IMAGES

BACKGROUND NOISE

Know your phone and know how to avoid unwelcome background noise.

Note, too, that some phone systems automatically cancel the *hold* facility after 20 or 30 seconds! Does yours?

TELEPHONE IMAGES

EFFECTIVE USE OF INFORMATION

As mentioned earlier, a customer can dial the same number on different occasions and be dealt with by entirely different locations. This shouldn't be a problem if there is up-to-date information on transaction history available for each customer at each location.

Accurate recording (and subsequent use) of information can lead to better customer service.

TELEPHONE IMAGES

EFFECTIVE USE OF INFORMATION

Case Study

A customer who had cause to complain about his mobile phone's lack of signal abroad, in countries he had specified he wanted to use it, eventually got a supervisor from the network provider to agree to upgrade the phone without surcharge fee and on the existing contract. The supervisor had promised to contact the customer's phone shop to authorise the upgrade.

When this authorisation failed to turn up the customer called the network provider again on the same customer service number and asked for the supervisor. A different man came on and told the customer there was no record on the system of any discussion with the *alleged supervisor. Such authorisation would never have been agreed*. All of which called the customer a liar!

In fact there was not even a record of the customer's previous complaints and request for roaming services. The most the organisation's network supervisor would admit was that the earlier call could have been diverted to any one of a number of locations.

When that customer's contract came up for renewal, guess what he did?!

BAD EXPERIENCES

Turn a bad experience into a good one through good customer service.

No doubt, we can all cite examples of bad customer service and occasions when, as in the previous example, we've decided not to use a particular supplier ever again.

Research tells us that if we receive bad service we will tell about twenty-six people of our experience in glorious technicolor! They, in turn, will tell their friends.

We only tell about nine people of good service we have received!

Therefore it is essential that we turn a customer's bad experience into a good one.

TAKING OPPORTUNITY FROM A COMPLAINT

Always:

- Follow up in writing (e-mail) any phone conversation you have with a customer.
- Answer letters by the appropriate means. Is it best to reply by letter, e-mail, fax or phone? Consider which medium is the correct one. If you need to offer a quick solution a phone call will sound and be received better than an impersonal e-mail.
- Answer e-mails within 24 hours.
- Accept responsibility.
- Say *sorry* – the Four As principle (see opposite).
- Record and analyse complaints to improve service.

But be careful what you measure:

- Quantity – is just a numbers game.
- Quality – can be explored by looking at the nature, severity, frequency.
- Time – time-scale and time taken when fixing the problem.
- Cost of fixing – must be measured in terms of opportunity lost, long-term customer loyalty and compensation paid.

TAKING OPPORTUNITY FROM A COMPLAINT

The Four As Principle

Anticipate That the customer is disappointed. Otherwise why would the customer call or e-mail you?

Apologise Say ***Sorry*** – it is the best five-letter word. If the customer complains, it is their gift to you and your chance to make the customer a long-term one. Ensure you say it early on, acknowledging that you're sorry for the inconvenience, anxiety or upset caused. This expresses sympathy and understanding without accepting blame! It costs nothing and can defuse 50% of the problems.

Analyse I realise that you are upset. *What can I do to put it right?*

Answer Do not wait for the person to ask for your name. Give it freely, first saying *I will deal with this personally*. One very large financial services organisation has as its slogan: *You'll know our name at X Bank!* All members of the organisation are encouraged to own problems.

SAYING *SORRY*

Problems will happen – it's the way you deal with them that wins or loses business.

SORRY is the hardest five-letter word but the most important! Acknowledge the feelings of the customer by phone fax, letter, e-mail or face-to-face!

Customers expect an organisation to accept responsibility and the individual, who receives the e-mail or phone call on its behalf, to take the flak or make the apology! As customers, we do not care where the blame lies in the organisation. All we know is that it does!

Always remember to under promise and over achieve.
For example, if you know you can deal with the problem in one hour allowing for unforeseen contingencies, tell the customer two hours. When you call or respond in one and a half hours, the customer will think you are great!

FOCUS ON RESOLVING PROBLEMS

It seems to be human nature to want to defend ourselves when under attack – a survival instinct! Unfortunately, it's not the way to survive in the commercial world.

Such an approach is concerned with focusing on the past and trying to rationalise events with reason. The problem is that it can amount to guesswork and merely falls under the label of *excuses*. **Never make excuses!** They show weakness, not strength.

Instead, focus your attention on the future rather than the past. The past cannot be changed as far as that customer is concerned. Looking to the future keeps your mind on resolving the problem, which is really why the customer has contacted you.

E-MAGES

Earlier, we identified that 55% of a message may be left to our imagination in the case of a telephone conversation. We saw that the person on the other end of the phone, whom we've never met, takes on facial characteristics and a dress-sense of our own creation! Our imagination has freedom to roam.

There are techniques that we reviewed to ensure that we give customers the impression of friendliness and professionalism. But how do we achieve this over the internet? What *e-mages* do we create for them?

Factors that contribute to an organisation's *e-mage* are:

- Scope of Home Page
- Language
- Ease of navigation
- Quality and quantity of information gathering

E-MAGES

SCOPE OF HOME PAGE

The Home Page is very much the shop window of e-commerce.

When we go shopping we are encouraged to explore a shop because of its window display, its name, a referral or merely the scale of it. The very same factors are just as likely to dissuade us from popping in!

Do we want our website to be a department store where customers can get most of what they might want if they put in the effort to look around? Or, would we prefer to be a specialist shop where the customer can go straight to the assistant and ask for the particular product or service?

If, as a shopper, we don't know which of the products or services best fits our needs, we would expect expert or, at least, knowledgeable advice from the assistant. The architecture of the website must support this option if people are not to leave the 'shop' in frustration or confusion.

E-MAGES

LANGUAGE

The language of interaction in shops is direct, conversational and usually courteous. It is not long-winded, pompous and full of complex sentences. It is, after all, the spoken word.

Typical of the words and phrases used in shops are:

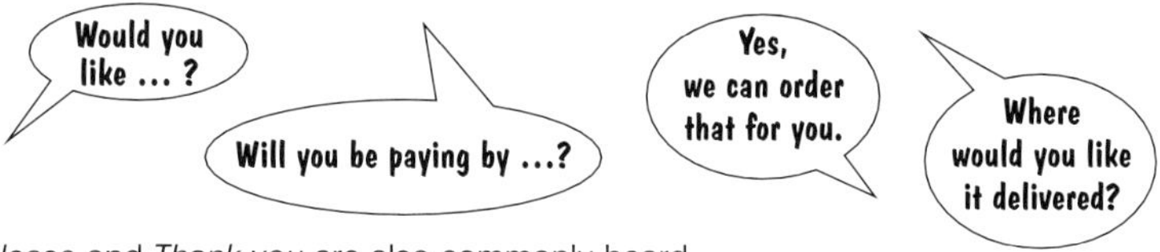

Please and *Thank you* are also commonly heard.

In contrast to the high street, the instructional or blunt language of most internet *pro-formae* is not conducive to putting the customer first. The system is seen as more important, yet it is still only a medium between buyer and seller. Virtual shopkeepers should follow the example of their high street counterparts.

E-MAGES

EASE OF NAVIGATION

Some people like to spend hours in department stores, wandering around the aisles, looking at what's available, possibly getting some exercise and keeping out of the rain. The longer a person spends in a shop does not, though, result in more money being spent. The shopper may be getting lost and indecisive owing to the choices available.

Avoid making shoppers' visits to your virtual shop tiresome and confusing. Provide clear signposts – using labels they'd recognise – and once the need is established, don't offer too many choices. Key words (*meta tags*) should be clearly distinguished so that any search engine used can find your site and appropriate web pages.

A trained salesperson will guide us with questions. These will help to confirm our needs and match the product or service to them. Brief customer responses to just two or three questions should therefore provide the navigation, rather than enforcing effort to plough through various (floor) levels and walkways.

NB Customers tend to browse at home, then purchase at work where the bandwidth is better. This leads to a lot of hits by non-buyers in the evenings and a lot of decisive purchases in office hours. This, however, could be affected by legislation governing the social use of e-mail at work.

E-MAGES

QUALITY & QUANTITY OF INFORMATION GATHERING

Customers expect to have to supply information during the course of a sale. They will, however, resent expending too much effort in doing so, particularly if it is not perceived as relevant or if it is information that they have given before.

When we looked at 'language', we saw the impact of the questioning style in bringing about a courteous, two-way exchange. Here, it is more to do with the obligatory form-filling before the system will allow us to process the sale any further.

Often form-filling on the internet smacks of impending mailshots, suggesting that the supplier is more interested in whom the mailing list can be sold to than in enhancing the service currently on offer. Thoughts of *big brother* may also be prompted. The upshot is that the customer puts forward any old information just to get the form out of the way.

To obtain genuine responses to your questionnaires, ensure that the information you seek is considered by the customer to be reasonable.

E-MAGES

QUALITY & QUANTITY OF INFORMATION GATHERING

We said earlier that you should avoid telling a customer who has reached the end of a telephone queue that they should have followed another route. Similarly, on the internet you should not put the customer to the trouble of filling out a long order form only for him or her to be told that the desired delivery date cannot be met.

Frustration and needless form-filling can be overcome by having a complementary search system operating in the background. For example, Carpricecheck.com takes your car requirement details and then, in the background, carries out the processing to find the best car price from dealers and web companies. It e-mails you back several minutes later. This simple approach means that you are not locked into a web screen for several minutes, and also means that you have the response in your inbox which is easy to access at a later date, if required.

NETIQUETTE

E-mail is powerful but is frequently misused and can paralyse an organisation if over-used. Here are some tips:

- Avoid *fire and forget.* Don't pass ownership of a problem with an e-mail. The problem is yours until someone else confirms they accept it.
- Only write things in an e-mail about a customer/colleague that you would say face-to-face (you never know who may see the e-mail, and you could be sued).
- Don't assign blame in an e-mail.
- Don't assume your e-mail is going to be read (or understood).
- Don't assume your e-mail is going to be read immediately. If it needs urgent consideration, follow up with a phone call.
- Consider carefully whom you copy e-mail to – you could annoy people by sending unnecessary e-mails.
- Consider carefully before copying e-mails to bosses of recipients – this can lead to an e-mail war.

NETIQUETTE

- Re-read your e-mail before sending.
- Beware of copyright and licensing laws when composing or forwarding your e-mails.
- Do use e-mail to record agreements reached. But remember, it's nearly always more effective to talk to someone, because you have two-way communication rather than one-way.
- Never put emotion into e-mails as all documents that are written in any form can be used as a legal document in a Court of Law! If you cannot meet the person face-to-face, use the phone to try and resolve the issues amicably!
- We forget that once committed to paper and sent, an e-mail lasts forever! Changes made during the process of communication may be ones that others have made without the knowledge of the originator. Avoid doing this, unless you make it clear you have made the change.

Tip: Don't negotiate by e-mail. It cannot easily give an accurate indication of intention and tone, and can inflame situations.

NETIQUETTE

PROBLEMS WITH E-MAILS

Most of us are poor typists and often make grammatical mistakes or use words out of context. For example, the phrase *This is not covered by our agreement with you* means, when included on an e-mail, that you deny the liability of the company you represent. However, by phone this could be viewed as stating the fall-back position, allowing an ex gratia payment (a payment without admitting liability) or free service to be offered as a sign of goodwill, thus binding the customer to you because of your consideration towards them.

E-mail is a great record-keeper of what has happened and/or been agreed. Negotiate by phone and follow up with an e-mail.

There is no acknowledgement with e-mail but there is an assumption made that it will be read and understood by the recipient!

LEGAL IMPLICATIONS

When using e-mail or phone take care over each and every communication as there may be a legal perspective.

E-mail

All correspondence by e-mail is actionable in law whether it is casual, social or legal in its content. It is strongly recommended that all e-mails have a legal disclaimer on all correspondence. This should comprise the:

- Confidential nature of the communication
- Limitation of reliance on the document by the recipient
- Scope of any advice given
- Contractual obligation entered into by the organisation

LEGAL IMPLICATIONS

Phone

By committing your organisation to a course of action with any customer or supplier, an employee may create a verbal and legally binding contract.

Each country has its own legislature and therefore laws in each country will be different. However, it is generally accepted that any document in the form of telephone notes, file notes made at the time of the call or e-mails, faxes or letters sent can be used as evidence of a contractual relationship.

MANAGEMENT ISSUES

POST HASTE

A particular issue for management to address is that a lot of dot.coms are poor at returning e-mails. This in turn leads to the customer phoning the call centre, which for the dot.com is even more expensive than answering the e-mail. Moreover, it reflects badly on the organisation and may well leave the customer venting his/her anger at the recipient – something the call centre needs to equip its staff to deal with properly. Worse still, there are incidents being reported of call centre staff becoming so stressed by the workload that some of them have broken down in tears while taking calls from irate customers.

Onyx research showed that approximately a quarter of websites interrogated with a business proposition failed to respond to an internet query. Another quarter took over five days to respond.

MANAGEMENT ISSUES

AUDIT LADDER

Use the rating scales on the next two pages to review your own organisation against the best practice approach of A1. How do **you** measure up?

It is possible that your organisation falls within more than one of the rating bands, indicating that certain parts of the overall approach are moving at different paces. Perhaps the system is getting all the attention and staff are being ignored for too long, or staff are doing their best but the internal processes are inhibiting them from giving customers what they need.

It is, of course, natural to focus separately on these aspects. However, just think where we'd be if we allowed that to happen all the time and we did everything in series rather than in parallel. There would be hi-tech aircraft on the runway but because pilot training had been overlooked during product development, there would be no one to fly them. Or no passengers to use them should marketing have been ignored at the appropriate time.

Unless you have already done so, now is your chance to:

- Identify how well you employ business intelligence
- Determine whether you are using best practice models for your staff development, and
- Establish just whom your systems are really there to help

AUDIT LADDER

Rating	Findings
A1	A CRM system has been in operation effectively for a minimum of three years. All staff have attained NVQ accreditation against customer service or call centre standards. Calls and e-mail responses are regularly monitored to check on and maintain standards. Systems and internal processes exceed customer needs and expectations
A	Customer information and transaction details are accurate and up-to-date, and accessible to all points of contact. All staff have undergone customer service training to attain in-house standards. Training needs are regularly reviewed for individuals and acted upon without undue delay. Systems and internal processes support customer needs and expectations.
B	Customer information and transaction details are up-dated regularly and are accessible in a format available to given contact points. Key staff have been trained in tailored telephone/written skills and systems as appropriate. Training needs are reviewed annually for job roles rather than for individuals. Systems and internal processes are consistent and support the needs of the organisation.

AUDIT LADDER

Rating	Findings
C	Customer information and transaction details are recorded haphazardly, according to the needs of the contact point, and are not available centrally. Basic training is provided at the outset or use of scripts is available. Staff are expected to use their initiative and report back on their own shortcomings. Systems and internal processes vary from points of contact and support the needs of the individual or department.
D	Only basic information is held about the customer and only specific transactions are recorded. Necessary skills/knowledge identified but no training provided. Poor performers are dismissed. Systems and internal processes vary from day-to-day and support the needs of the points of contact only.
E	Customers are identified by a number and transaction details are destroyed on a regular basis. Necessary skills/knowledge have not even been identified. Employee performance is not monitored. Systems and internal processes are virtually non-existent and mainly show that money is coming in.

MANAGEMENT ISSUES

CUSTOMER REASSURANCE

Many *clicks and mortar* organisations now exist. These are companies that have successfully integrated their *on-line virtual* existence with their *real world off-line* physical presence. They have the advantage of being able to sustain an *e-strategy* alongside their branch concept. Thus customers can either call into a branch or order via the website.

It is becoming evident that customers still like to have face-to-face contact. They want the opportunity to see and, if necessary, sample the goods before purchase.

Convenience for the sellers may not coincide with convenience for the customers! Customers, it would seem, miss the *market square* where, in a clearly defined area, there are many products to choose from, at affordable prices, all of which can be inspected before purchase.

How, then, would you provide the reassurance they seek, even down to letting them know which person to take items back to should a problem arise?

FACING THE CUSTOMER

The downside of internet shopping is its facelessness. It's all too easy to hide behind the terminal or telephone and dismiss the customer's cries for help or pass them off to another *agent* who is supposed to provide back-up support. (This term may indeed have originated from getting the customer's back up, as that's what support invariably does!)

Management should come out from behind the screens and familiarise itself with the Sales of Goods Act and other relevant legislation. It could be *face the customer* or *face the consequences!*

SETTING OUT YOUR STALL

As we saw overleaf, the customer has a perception of a market square – but how do you set out your stall? What do you want your market square to look like?

At inception, determine whether the call centre will:

- Log calls
- Service all queries, or
- Provide something between the two

Remember, there is a hidden cost in follow-up calls from customers (particularly where a disgruntled customer may call back repeatedly).

QUALITY NOT JUST QUANTITY

Beware the cost of cheating.

Sometimes call numbers and responses can be increased by one call centre member ringing another, and then immediately hanging up the phone. This speeds up the call rate and indicates that the *one and done* response is therefore perfect!

Don't become too reliant on the quantitative factors. It should be quality that matters.

DON'T RELY ON STATISTICS

Statistics should not be all that matters. After all, what do they really tell you?

A major insurance group restructured its branch network and put all of its *personal lines* business through a smaller number of regional customer service teams (CSTs). Staff were retrained so that they could deal with both household and motor insurance rather than just one class of business as before.

Each CST was then provided with telephone skills training for each of its team members. However, one regional CST manager felt that it was unnecessary as his team was already up to speed. He even had statistics to support his case, showing the volume of calls for each person and their typical duration. Eventually he acceded to the external training consultant spending a morning with the team, listening unobtrusively and recording live calls.

DON'T RELY ON STATISTICS

The evidence was damning! Customers were ringing up and asking for the Motor Underwriting department (as was their previous reference) only to hear the team member say *We don't have one any more!* Imagine the ensuing confusion, not to mention fear and uncertainty, it left in the minds of the customers. The situation was exacerbated by the team's unfamiliarity in dealing with a new system and live customers at the same time! Needless to say, it could all have been avoided with the correct training.

The call statistics proffered by the misguided manager showed that the call volume was high – but only because there were lots of confused and worried customers ringing back!

Tip: Internal labels are for internal consumption. For customers, use labels they will recognise.

QUALITY MEASURES

Statistics with quality measures are concerned with ensuring that customers feel they have been listened to and cared for. The quantitative approach is to satisfy internal demands only and is frequently unrealistic.

- 30 calls per hour or 10 e-mails per hour. Merely quantity, not quality.
- How many repeat customers do you have each month? Quality, not merely quantity.

What gets measured gets done.

OFFSHORING…'A PASSAGE TO INDIA'

Outsourcing is one of the most important trends affecting world business today. It allows companies to focus on their core business, and can vary from straightforward voice services and systems integrators to full call centre implementations. The choice is overwhelming, with over 150 outsourcers in the UK alone and a fast growing supply of labour and technology offshore.

India already hosts airline, banking, insurance, health and legal operations for Western-based industry. According to a study by consultants McKinsey, some 20 per cent of the Fortune 1000 companies outsource to the subcontinent. American Express, Citibank, HSBC and Standard Chartered all have call centre operations in India, and the offshoring market is expected to increase by 57% by 2006.

MANAGEMENT ISSUES

OFFSHORING

THE TOP FOUR

INDIA

Advantages:

- Low-cost labour pool
- Large graduate numbers (2 million/year)
- Skilled population (80% English speaking)
- Good English language skills
- Strong in all areas of offshoring
- Equidistant between European/American time zones

Disadvantages:

- Strong accent in some regions makes voice recognition hard
- Highly competitive (salaries likely to increase to retain staff)
- Threat of new tax laws

PHILIPPINES

Advantages:

- Government focused on an e-services hub in customer contact centres/medical transcription/business processes/out-sourcing/shared financial services/software development
- Good for voice processes (recognition systems)

Disadvantages:

- Fewer graduates than India/China (approx 380,000/year)

CHINA

Advantages:

- Very low cost of staff ($200 per month)
- Ideal for back-office based processing within limited language capability
- Government focus on manufacturing and high-tech sectors

Disadvantages:

- Lower language capabilities than other Asian countries
- Fewer graduates than India (approx 850,000/year with 50% English speaking)

SOUTH AFRICA

Advantages:

- Skilled population with excellent English
- Similar culture/business practices to Western countries (eg: Anglo American financial services sector)
- Time zone same as Europe

Disadvantages:

- Lower graduate population
- Average wage ($1500-1800/month) higher than in Asia

CROSS-SELLING

Cross-selling is the opportunity to offer your customers another product or service from across your business range, in addition to the one they have already purchased.

For example, Direct Line is able to cross-sell Green Flag roadside assistance to its car insurance customers. Its aim is to transfer the same customer interaction it carries out at its call centre to internet-enabled phones and interactive TV. To achieve this it must be able to identify high value customers - who are profitable, who would otherwise go elsewhere, and who are interested in a new product.

Tip: You need to decide whether to spend 20 seconds or 20 minutes with a customer. Remember the Pareto principle (80:20 Rule): probably 20% of your customers buy/use 80% of your services or products.

MANAGEMENT ISSUES

HR ISSUES

Within the call centre and internet environment the quality of life varies enormously for staff. It depends upon product market, local labour market, and the company's HR practices.

Where building a strong customer relationship is important, there needs to be a high commitment to the call centre staff in order to reduce staff turnover so that relationships can be maintained.

Where processing transactions is more important than relationships, then empowerment tends to be low, staff are tightly managed and personnel turnover might be higher. This environment is often commodity based, and roles may be automated using voice recognition systems or websites.

BRAAN, which operates call centres for Virgin Mobile, Sainsbury's and Fiat, varies its staffing practices. For short-term transactional interactions with customers, such as the response to an advertising campaign, it uses new recruits and agency staff on short contracts. By contrast, it uses experienced permanent staff dedicated solely to one client for long-term contracts, those that require relationship building and understanding brand values (eg: running financial services).

E-SSENTIAL TRAINING

Training and development progression plan

The progression plan on the following pages can be used as a *template* for identifying the skills likely to be required at each level of the organisation. View it as a ladder, on which the individual rises, acquiring new skills at each new rung and bringing with him or her the skills acquired at the lower rung or rungs.

For convenience, we've grouped the skills in our plan under traditional labels (see column 1). A best practice approach will define standards of performance expected within each label or job role, enabling you to identify easily if a person is performing to the required level. It will also help you to design training solutions that focus on outcomes needed.

Too often training is reactive. Don't hold off and weep, instead prepare people and reap!

E-SSENTIAL TRAINING

Training and development progression plan

Level	Key Responsibilities	Essential Skills	Skills Required by some Staff	Support Skills
Senior Management Call Centre & Branch Managers	Corporate policy and strategy Planning/ Directing	Strategic planning, Competitive analysis, Identifying need for change		
Middle Management	Achieving results through others	Project management, Managing change, Budgeting & finance, Stress management, Man management, Leadership, Presentation skills, Problem solving, Influencing skills, Managing meetings, Team building	Selection interviewing	CRM project management
Sales Force	Managing the business		Counselling	
Relationship Managers			Selling	

E-SSENTIAL TRAINING

Training and development progression plan

Level	Key Responsibilities	Essential Skills	Skills Required by some Staff	Support Skills
Technical or Supervisory Field Service Help Desk	Taking responsibility for the task, the team or self	Interpersonal skills, Time management, Motivation, Coaching, Appraisal	Technical report writing	Report functionality of CRM system
Senior Clerical or Administrative Accounts Sales Office	Advanced processing Dealing with clients and more complex enquiries	Assertiveness, Handling complaints, Effective letter writing		Use of CRM communications management
Clerical Call Centre staff	Processing Dealing with non-complex enquiries	Telephone techniques, Active listening, Being an effective team member, Office practices		Keyboard skills, Use of telephone system, Use of CRM database

CALL CENTRE CAPACITY

Don't make the mistake of thinking that because you offer an internet service you can reduce telephone call centre capacity. Unless you are sure that you have resolved:

- Poor web design
- Lengthy downloads
- Poor response times
- Poor search facilities
- Limited product information

Everyone now feels they've got to have a website but most don't adapt it for customer needs nor service it adequately. So instead of being an alternative route, a website instigates even more calls to the centre.

MANAGEMENT ISSUES

SECURITY

To protect customer information and credit details, an organisation must:

- Build in security to design (BS7799)
- Plan for its system to be swamped
- Check audit logs
- Use firewalls (electronic barriers between your network and outside world)

SECURITY

Despite high profile publicity of security breaches (eg: the 'love bug') the number of breaches is increasing. Management needs to identify the objectives of the e-business operation and assess the security risk, so that it can build in security from the outset.

Use 4 steps for security:

1. Establish the identity of the customer
2. Legally bind yourself, as the seller, and the customer to the transaction
3. Ensure a high level of encryption
4. Check that the information sent is identical to that received

MANAGEMENT ISSUES

THE FUTURE

E-customer service is here to stay. Current developments with WAP (Wireless Application Protocol) will give call centres the opportunity to generate event-driven messages directly to customers. You may receive a text message when your insurance is due for renewal, and it may be possible to enter into a binding contract through the exchange of such Short Messaging Systems (SMSs).

Wireless subscribers now outnumber wired subscribers in the domestic market. It is anticipated that wireless users worldwide will reach 1.5 billion within the next few years (Strategy Analytics) with 40% of B2C calls being made via mobile systems (Gartner). Mobile e-commerce is likely to become m-commerce.

Advances in digital technology have already brought opportunities for transactions to take place through interactive TV sets, which offers a potentially huge audience.

Ultimately, this new revolution will allow organisations to conduct business with the customer through any channel, at any time, in any language, and in any currency. However, the greater convenience of communication methods and wider accessibility between seller and consumer will provide more customer choice. Will customers choose you?

JARGON BUSTERS

B2B (Business to Business) encompasses commercial activity between one business and another and is a frequently used term for internet business transactions.

B2C (Business to Consumer) encompasses commercial activity between a business (supplier) and a customer (domestic rather than business).

CRM (Customer Relationship Management) systems are packaged software solutions for **front** office functions such as customer contact, sales, marketing, accounts receivable, etc. As implied in the name, they include the **customer** in the business processes being managed. Examples include Siebel and Clarify. Several ERP suppliers are now also extending their applications to cover some aspects of CRM.

Clicks and mortar organisations are companies that have successfully integrated their on-line virtual existence with their real world off-line physical presence.

JARGON BUSTERS

Cross-selling is the opportunity to offer your customer another product or service from across your business range, in addition to the one they have already purchased.

ERP (Enterprise Resource Planning) systems are packaged software solutions for **back** office functions such as accounts payable, payroll, human resources, financials and manufacturing. They often include the **supplier** in the business processes being managed. Examples include SAP, Oracle, Peoplesoft, Baan and JD Edwards.

Firewall is a gatekeeper (computer) that sits between the internet and your private network. It protects the private network by filtering traffic to and from the internet, based on policies that you define. You can use the firewall to define who can get on to your network and when.

Hyperlinks allow you to link web pages and documents together.

Up-selling is when you aim to get the customer to buy a higher level of the same product or service (an up-grade) to meet their needs better.

USEFUL WEBSITES & PUBLICATIONS

Client/Server Survival Guide, Orfali, Harkey & Edwards
The Customer Service Pocketbook, Tony Newby & Sean McManus, Management Pocketbooks
The E-commerce Pocketbook, Will Rowan, Management Pocketbooks
Financial Times
People Management Journal
The Telesales Pocketbook, Peter Wyllie, Management Pocketbooks

Useful websites to access training and service information:

- oftel.org.com
- zed.com
- FT.com

About the Author

Mike Applegarth

Mike has been a training professional for 25 years, with over 20 of those spent as a consultant. His assignments have involved him in projects within a range of industries from insurance to petrochemicals, and his clients are within the private and public sectors and amongst charitable institutions.

He specialises in auditing the effectiveness of the training function and in producing tailored solutions to team performance and development issues, and he has implemented competence-based frameworks for use in employee recruitment and assessment.

He is the author of *How To Take A Training Audit*, first printed in July 1991 as a leader in the Kogan Page Practical Trainer Series.

Contact: Mike can be contacted at Applegarth Professional Training, Manfield House, Collins Gardens, Ash, Surrey GU12 6EP.
Tel: +44 (0) 1252 338517 or email to mapple@globalnet.co.uk.

About the Author

Adrian Guttridge, BSc (Hons) FBCS, CEng, CITP
Currently a director with financial services group Abbey, Adrian has over 20 years' experience in information technology and business process outsourcing. Most of his career has been spent working for service companies such as Logica, Data Logic, Accenture and Marlborough Stirling. He has worked in several industry sectors with organisations as diverse as National Westminster Bank, the industrial gases group BOC, the utility company Seeboard, and financial services companies Prudential and Abbey.

Adrian has extensive call centre experience. In the late nineties he was the Service Implementation Manager for the call centre and back-office re-engineering at Seeboard. In 2000, as Head of Service Management at Prudential, he had line responsibility for re-engineering the IT help desks which served approximately 10,000 users. In 2003, he was the CEO for a joint venture between Egg and Marlborough Stirling, providing mortgage business process services to several mortgage lenders, which included call-centre capability. Adrian is also a member of the Institute of Directors.

Contact: Adrian can be contacted at adrianguttridge@aol.com

About the Author

Keith Posner, LLB FCIPD

Keith began his professional training career over 17 years ago at Nationwide Building Society. He then joined Cornhill Insurance and managed the specialist training function on their business process re-engineering project team.

Keith and his wife Sian formed Positive Perspective nine years ago. Their team of consultants specialise in one-to-one executive coaching, and designing and delivering a wide range of individually tailored training programmes, including: *Business Planning* and *Project Management, Stress Management, Life Balance, Leadership & Motivation, Selling & Negotiation Skills, Management of Change, Team Building, Career Development Centres* and *Communication & Empowerment.*

Positive Perspective's client base includes managing directors, partners and senior managers from prominent global and national companies, notably within the utilities, financial and service sectors. With Mike Applegarth he has written two other pocketbooks, on empowerment and project management.

Contact: Keith can be contacted at: Positive Perspective, The Coach House, Henfold Lane, South Holmwood, Dorking, Surrey RH5 4NX Tel: +44 (0)1306 88 89 90
E-mail: keithp@pospers.co.uk www.positiveperspective.co.uk

ORDER FORM

Your details

Name ______________________

Position ______________________

Company ______________________

Address ______________________

____

____

Telephone ______________________

Fax ______________________

E-mail ______________________

VAT No. (EC companies) ______________________

Your Order Ref ______________________

Please send me:

	No. copies
The Call Centre Customer Care Pocketbook	
The ______________ Pocketbook	
The ______________ Pocketbook	
The ______________ Pocketbook	
The ______________ Pocketbook	

Order by Post

MANAGEMENT POCKETBOOKS LTD

LAUREL HOUSE, STATION APPROACH, ALRESFORD,
HAMPSHIRE SO24 9JH UK

Order by Phone, Fax or Internet

Telephone: +44 (0)1962 735573
Facsimile: +44 (0)1962 733637
E-mail: sales@pocketbook.co.uk
Web: www.pocketbook.co.uk

MANAGEMENT POCKETBOOKS

Customers in USA should contact:
Stylus Publishing, LLC, 22883 Quicksilver Drive,
Sterling, VA 20166-2012
Telephone: 703 661 1581 or 800 232 0223
Facsimile: 703 661 1501 E-mail: styluspub@aol.com